PAUL WALSH MEMORIAL LECTURE 7

The O'Donnells at War in the 1640s and Early 1650s

Eoin Mac Cárthaigh

Scoil an Léinn Cheiltigh, Ollscoil Mhá Nuad
School of Celtic Studies, Maynooth University

LÉACHT CHUIMHNEACHÁIN AN BHREATHNAIGH 7

ISBN- 9798362922078

Copyright © 2022 Eoin Mac Cárthaigh

Eagarthóir na Sraithe/General Editor
Elizabeth Boyle

Arna fhoilsiú ag Scoil an Léinn Cheiltigh, Ollscoil Mhá Nuad
Published by the School of Celtic Studies, Maynooth University

The O'Donnells at War in the 1640s and Early 1650s[1]

I am very grateful for the invitation to give this lecture, and for the opportunity to celebrate Paul Walsh's abiding legacy eighty years after his death. I need not detail that legacy here, but he had a lifelong interest in the fortunes of the Ó Domhnaill dynasty, and his edition of *Beatha Aodha Ruaidh Uí Dhomhnaill* is undoubtedly one of his finest achievements. It has also left me personally indebted to Fr Walsh, as a chapter entitled 'Poems to Calvach Ruadh Ó Domhnaill', in the second volume, was the starting point many years ago of my postgraduate research.[2]

The focus of what follows is Ó Domhnaill participation in the war that began in 1641, but a brief overview of the dynasty in the first half of the seventeenth century will help to clarify who was available to take part in the war.

The demise of the line of Aodh son of Maghnas

Aodh Ruadh son of Aodh son of Maghnas was leader of the family and ruler of Tír Chonaill at the opening of the seventeenth century. He led his men to Kinsale in 1601 and afterwards embarked for Spain to seek military aid, dying there in 1602. His brother, Rudhraighe, took his place and became first Earl of Tír Chonaill after making peace with the Crown in 1603. Rudhraighe and another brother, Cathbharr, subsequently fled to the Continent in 1607 in the 'flight of the earls' and both died the next year in Rome, to where the leaders of that ill-fated expedition had been side-lined.

---

[1]This lecture was delivered on 16 December 2021 at Maynooth University.

[2] Walsh (1948–57, 2: 149–155); both volumes were published after Walsh's death, having been prepared for the press by Colm Ó Lochlainn. All dates below have the year beginning on 1 January, rather than 25 March. All text is quoted as it appears in print except that macrons are replaced silently with lengthmarks and italicised text with Roman.

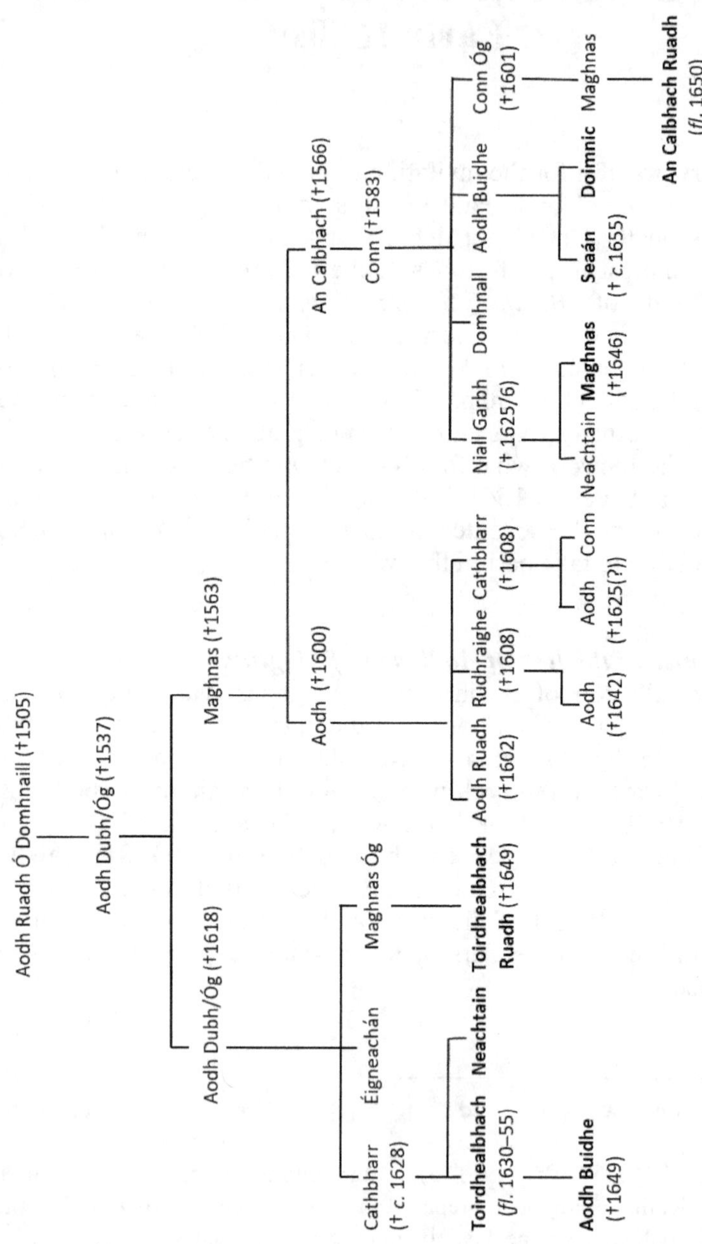

Aodh Ruadh Ó Domhnaill (†1505)
Aodh Dubh/Óg (†1537)
Maghnas (†1563)
Aodh Dubh/Óg (†1618)
An Calbhach (†1566)
Aodh (†1600)
Conn (†1583)
Conn Óg (†1601)
Maghnas
An Calbhach Ruadh (fl. 1650)
Aodh Buidhe
Niall Garbh
Domhnall
Seaán († c.1655)
Doimnic
Neachtain
Maghnas (†1646)
Cathbharr (†1608)
Rudhraighe (†1608)
Aodh Ruadh (†1602)
Aodh Conn (†1625(?))
Aodh (†1642)
Cathbharr († c. 1628)
Éigneachán
Maghnas Óg
Neachtain
Toirdhealbhach Ruadh (†1649)
Toirdhealbhach (fl. 1630–55)
Aodh Buidhe (†1649)

Their sons, Aodh son of Rudhraighe and Aodh son of Cathbharr, were brought up in Louvain and, in time, entered the Spanish service. Aodh son of Rudhraighe came to be recognised as the second Earl of Tír Chonaill. He was refused permission to return to Ireland at the outbreak of hostilities in 1641 and died fighting for the Spanish king in 1642.[3] Aodh son of Cathbharr predeceased him, perhaps in 1625 at the siege of Breda, but was certainly dead by 1631, the year of writing of the Book of the O'Conor Don, which originally contained a poem sympathising with an aunt of his on his death.[4] A younger brother of his, Conn son of Cathbharr, was left in Ireland in 1607 and brought up under the supervision of the colonial authorities. He was sent to London in 1626, with the commendation that he 'has always been a Protestant and is loyal',[5] but apparently fled to the Continent later that year.[6] I have no further record of him, and he appears to have played no part in the war that began in 1641, leaving this branch of the dynasty absent from the conflict.

Branches surviving in Ireland into the 1640s

Protagonists active in Ireland in the 1640s belonged to two branches granted lands in the Ulster Plantation, which followed the 1607 'flight'.

Niall Garbh (son of Conn) and his brothers had rebelled against Aodh Ruadh, and one of the brothers, Conn Óg, died in that rebellion in 1601. I have located no record of Domhnall or of Aodh Buidhe after 1615, when they were implicated in a conspiracy against Crown interests.[7] Niall Garbh himself died in the Tower of London in 1625 or 1626.[8] His son, Neachtain, was also held there and the Four Masters say he died there.[9] Another

---

[3] For a general account of his life, see Jennings (1941: passim). For further details on his final years, see Breatnach (1994–95: passim).

[4] The poem is *Tinn liom do mhaoith, a Mháire* by Uilliam Óg Mac an Bhaird (Mac Cárthaigh 2012); see p. 162 of that edition for dating.

[5] Mahaffy 1900: 132.

[6] See Casway (1987: 32); Mac Cárthaigh (2012: 163).

[7] See Russell and Prendergast (1880: 42, 52–3).

[8] The year of his death is given as 1625 in the elegy *Bean do lámhaigheadh leith Cuinn* (Walsh 1933: 27–52, q. 59) but as 1626 in 'Oiris oirdhearca Tíre Conaill' (Walsh 1948–57, 2: 87–97, §54).

[9] O Donovan (1856, 6: 2364). Walsh (1948–57, 2: 196–197) refers to a mention of Neachtain in 1623, but has no later date for him, and nor have I.

son, Maghnas son of Niall Garbh, played a prominent role in the war, and a nephew and grandnephew of Niall Garbh also receive mention in wartime sources – Seaán (son of Aodh Buidhe) and An Calbhach Ruadh (grandson of Conn Óg).

Members of another branch of the family also fought in the war. These were Toirdhealbhach son of Cathbharr son of Aodh Dubh/Óg, his brother Neachtain, his son Aodh Buidhe and his first cousin Toirdhealbhach Ruadh.

1641

One of the first sources we have for the war in Donegal is a poem of incitement, of which I give here the scribal introduction and the first quatrain:

> Uilliam Og mac Uilliam Oig M[h]eic an Bháird do rinne an dan-sa ag greasacht fhear nEireann et aga ccomhairliughadh im shnadhmad[h] rer oile in énbháidh charthannaigh et in énaonta a ttús an chogaidh oirdheirc ·1641·

> Dia libh, a uaisle Éireann!
> Tógb[h]aidh tosach caithréimeann!
> Tánaig uair d'f[h]óirithin cáigh;
> róimhithidh an uain d'f[h]agháil.

> Uilliam Óg son of Uilliam Óg Mac an Bhaird composed this poem inciting the men of Ireland and advising them to join with each other in one friendly alliance and in unity at the beginning of the famous war, 1641:

> God be with you, O nobles of Ireland! Make a beginning to triumphs! The time has come to help everyone. It is high time [for you] to get the opportunity.[10]

While the poem is addressed to all of the nobility of Ireland, both Gaelic and Old English (urging them to fight *pro Deo* and *pro patria*, but making no mention of fighting *pro rege*), its author probably belonged to the Co. Donegal Mac an Bhaird family, and the closing quatrains are directed at Co. Donegal nobles:

> A uaisle che[i]néal gConaill,
> a iolchraobha a héanchrobhaing,
> ní mín do gríosadh bhar ngoimh
> dá dtíosadh dhíbh a dhíoghail.

---

[10] Mac Cárthaigh (2002).

> O nobles of Conall's race, O manifold branches from one cluster,
> your venom was not incurred with impunity if you could exact
> revenge for it. (q. 44)

At least some of the O'Donnells were active from the very early
days of the rising. A report from the Fanad peninsula dated 27
October 1641, a few days after the outbreak of hostilities, names
Toirdhealbhach son of Cathbharr:

> I fear arresting of the O'Donells in this part of the country.
> Turlogh McKraffer has brought a great many men out of these
> parts, and is now with the O'Nealls, who committed the reported
> mischiefs.[11]

Toirdhealbhach is reported to be cooperating with Maghnas son of
Niall Garbh the following spring in an attack on Sir Ralph Gore's
castle at Magherabeg near Donegal town:

> the rebels mustered new forces, and with assistance of Colonell
> Manus O Donnell, and Colonell Turlogh, Mac Caffrye O Donnell,
> they besieged my Colonels castle, he being gone over the
> mountaines for ammunition, the rebels fired some out-houses, but
> were beaten off with losse of twenty men, who attempted to burne
> the gate.[12]

A contemporary pamphlet praises Sir William Stewart's efforts at
the end of 1642 to confront Toirdhealbhach and his allies in the
Fanad district:

> Sir William (getting notice that the Rebels of Fanet and Tarman,
> were under the leading of Tirlagh Mac Caffer, and some of the
> chiefe of the Met-Swynes, and O Galghonors, setled somewhat
> securely neere the head of Mulroy) commanded 7 of his
> Companies to make a nights march towards them ...[13]

Both Toirdhealbhach and Maghnas are implicated in an
unsuccessful ambush in Co. Sligo in another hostile account dated
15 May 1643:

---

[11] Letter from Éireamhón Mac Suibhne, Justice of the Peace, Ray, Co.
Donegal (Mahaffy 1901: 344).
[12] Statement by Lieutenant Colonel Audley Mervyn, 4 June 1642, Gilbert
(1879–80, 1/2: 470).
[13] Anon. (1643b: 1).

> And as we marched homewards with our Prey an Ambush of 400, or 500, Ulster Rebels, was laid for us, which men belonged to Mannus mac Neal, Garve O Donnel, Torilagh Roe O Boyl, Torilagh mac Caffry O Donnel, with a many of the O Gallachours, who thought themselves so strong, as some of their prisoners did report, That when they saw my Party marching, they said, they would be but a break-fast to them.[14]

Both also receive mention in the 1641 depositions from Co. Donegal. A deposition taken in late 1642 lists 'Tirlagh Mc Caffir Ó Donnell of Tullifarney gent a Captain' among the insurgents.[15] Another, taken in March 1643, alleges that the deponent's servants handed over some of his 'Cattle … horses & howsholdgoodes' to 'the Rebell Manus Ó Donnelle whose father Surnell Garrow o Donnelle dyed in the towne [*recte* towre]' and names 'the said Manus Ó Donnell' as one of the 'principall Rebells in the presente Action in this Kingdome'.[16]

Maghnas son of Niall Garbh

Mentions by name of O'Donnells in hostile sources are sporadic at best, so we are lucky to have an account of Maghnas's exploits in Gofraidh Óg Mac an Bhaird's poem, *As truagh cor chríche Banbha*.[17] This apologia for Maghnas's actions, composed after his death, is a useful (and equally partisan) counterbalance to pamphlets and letters extolling his enemies. For instance, contrast what the poet has to say about the Magherabeg attack with the hostile account given above:

> Do bhí bhós ar beagán cruidh
> ar ndódh dhaingein an dúnaidh
> an Mhachaire Bheag uaidh as;
> beag do-chuaidh tar a chomas.

> Furthermore, Magherabeg was left with few cattle by him after the stronghold of the fortress was burned; little was beyond his ability. (q. 24)

The poem offers a different perspective on ensuing events too. When Gore returned to Magherabeg, he and his fellow officers decided to leave only a small garrison there and to move everyone

---

[14] Anon. (1645: 50–51).
[15] Clarke *et al.* (2014: 243; see further 245).
[16] Clarke *et al.* (2014: 243–4).
[17] Mac Cárthaigh (2017).

else, including many refugees, northwards to more secure quarters in Raphoe. In order to do so, they would have to pass through the pass of Barnesmore, and they were ambushed there on 16 March 1642, as recounted by a fellow officer of Gore's, Sir Robert Stewart:

> wee discovered the enimie, who charged us in vann rere and both flankes att once, being obscured in the bushes till wee were so far ingaged. It pleased God att our first incounter wee beat of the partie opposing our vann and intertained on very hott fight for three hours time till all our unserviceable people and theire baggage were past. In conclusion wee routed them ...[18]

The poet states the opposite:

> Lá brisde an B[h]earnasa Móir
> ar Galluibh na ngníomh n-éccóir,
> do thuill barr tar chrú cConaill;
> rú ní[o]r am uraghuill.

> The day of the Barnesmore rout of the foreigners of the unjust deeds, he surpassed [the rest of] Conall's bloodline; it was no time to negotiate with them. (q. 25)

Maghnas took part in a follow-up campaign which culminated, in June 1642, in the battle of Glenmaquin, a defeat for the side he was fighting on. Here is an account giving an enemy perspective:

> The next Boute the Irish and British had in Ulster was at a place called Glommaquin in the County of Dungall, whither Sir Phelim O'Neill and O'Cahan, their chief Commanders marched with about 4,000 men. Which the British hearing, under the Command of Sir Robert Stewart, an old Soldier, entrenched themselves in Night time, but had not time to make it full Breast high before Morning, when the Irish appeared close to them, and sent a Brigade under the Command of Alexander MacColla MacDonnell, a stoute brave Fellow (under the command of Mount Rose afterwards in Scotland) who charged up alone to the work but was shot, and after a very smart skirmish the Irish fell back, and took the Retreat, where many were slain, and with much ado O'Cahan brought off MacDonnell in a Horse-Litter.[19]

---

[18] 'A true and breife accompt of the services done by the seaven British regiments and troopes raised in the kingdome of Ireland ...', Fane (1888: 299).

[19] *The history of the warr of Ireland ... By a British officer ...*, Hogan (1873: 23–24).

The poet makes no claim that the 'Irish' side was victorious but credits Maghnas with staying to the end and, in contradiction of a detail in the account just given, with being Alasdair mac Colla's rescuer:

> As Gleann Me[ic] Cuinn do-chuaidh lais
> clú mór ar a chéim chonntais;
> le deireadh deabhtha do an
> gach deighfhear dearbhtha [...].

> Mac Colla Chiotaigh na lann
> rug leis d'aimhdheóin eachtrann –
> nuaineim[h] an f[h]eadhma ar an fhior –
> ar guailnibh feardha féinneadh.

> Great fame for his deed of [great] account accompanied him out of Glenmaquin; every proven [...] good man stayed until the end of the fighting.

> Seized afresh by martial ardour, [and] despite foreigners, he brought [the injured] Mac Colla Chiotaigh of the blades [off the battlefield] on the manly shoulders of warriors. (qq. 29–30)

In the early days of the rising, the O'Donnells and their allies had failed to take the major strongholds but had gained control over much of the countryside. Now, however, even that became untenable, and Maghnas is praised for managing to withdraw with his herds intact:

> Rug ceat[h]ra a chríche féin
> d'aimhdheóin Gall na ngníomh n-aigmhéil –
> beag do threóruibh an mhín mhir –
> go Tír Eóg[h]ain ar éigin.

> Despite the foreigners of the fierce deeds, he brought the livestock of his own territory to Tyrone with difficulty – a little [example] of the skills of this animated gentleman. (q. 32)

This was of crucial strategic importance in a war that came to be characterised by the livestock and people following behind the army as it moved around the country, both for the supply of the army and for the protection of the people and livestock.[20]

---

[20] For a good example of this, see quatrains 24–31 of *Mo mhallacht ort, a shaoghail*, Mac Cárthaigh (2013).

Maghnas after Donegal

The exodus from Co. Donegal marked more than just a geographical shift in Ó Domhnaill actions. The rising in Ulster was floundering at this stage but was transformed by Eóghan Ruadh Ó Néill's return to Ireland in July 1642. *Síol nDálaigh* (the O'Donnells) are counted among those present at Clones in August when Eóghan was made general of the Ulster army.[21]

Gofraidh Óg's poem allows us to follow Maghnas's movements over the next few years, telling us, for instance, that he fought in Co. Mayo (quatrain 35) and in Co. Fermanagh (quatrains 36–37). In Mayo, he may have been taking part in the Earl of Castlehaven's 1644 campaign there. We know from another source that 1,500 Ulstermen fought under Castlehaven in Munster in the following year:

> Do gabhadh la Iarla Caisil-haven Lios Mór Mo Choda. Do bhean a' boile do Shíol mBriain ... 'sdo bheansat naoi [n]garasdon do Bharún Inis Í Chuinn; agus bhí cúig céad déag Ultach san [t]sluagh soin.[22]

> Lismore, Co. Waterford, was taken by the Earl of Castlehaven from the O Brien people ... They also captured nine garrisoned towns from Baron Inchiquin. That army included one thousand five-hundred Ulstermen.[23]

As truagh cor chríche Banbha makes clear that Maghnas was among them:

> Ní[o]r sheas a dheaghd[h]aingne do
> Lios Móraolta Mo Choda
> go b[h]fua[i]r thiar dá aimhdheóin é,
> taibhgheó[i]r ler m[h]ian a[n] mhoichré.

> Limewashed Lismore's substantial strength did not withstand this enforcer who liked an early morning [raid], with the result that he captured it, over in the west, despite resistance. (q. 43)

Indeed, the figure of 1,500 is in the same range as numbers which will be seen below for a regiment under another O'Donnell, and a good part of the Ulster detachment on this Munster campaign may well have been under Maghnas's command.

---

[21] *Cín lae Uí Mhealláin*, Ó Donnchadha (1931: 16).
[22] *Cín lae Uí Mealláin*, Ó Donnchadha (1931: 35).
[23] Translation by Charles Dillon (1995–96: 174).

Maghnus Ó Domhnaill mac Néill Ghairbh is named as one of Eóghan Ruadh's colonels at the battle of Benburb in June 1646,[24] and his death there receives mention in various contemporary sources:

> Lost of the Irish side, colonel Manus Mc Neale, Garve O Donnell, slain; ...[25]

> The Irish lost onely there of note Colonell Manus McNeylle, Garane O'Donnell[26]

> Do marbhadh Maghnus Úa Domhnaill, mac Néill Ghairbh, agus ...[27]

> Ex Catholicis non nisi septuaginta caesos, et centum fuisse vulneratos tradit Nuncius, sed, excepto Magno O'Donello ...[28]

Not least, of course, in Gofraidh Óg's elegy on him:

> Lá an m[h]órchatha san Bheinn Buirb,
> dob adhbhal échta a órchuilg,
> ag drud fan ágh gan fhuireach
> go dtug ár na n-allmhuireach.

> An lá-soin – níor lag an ghoimh –
> torchuir airsidh f[h]óid Fhion[n]tuin;
> ó ló céile cláir Uladh
> do-cháidh Éire ó [a]naghal.

> The day of the great battle in Benburb, awesome were the feats of his golden blade, approaching the fray without delay so that he wreaked slaughter on the foreigners.

> That day – it was no faint anguish – the veteran of Fionntan's land fell; since the day the spouse of Ulster's plain died, Ireland has become unprotected. (qq. 45–46)

---

[24] *Cín lae Uí Mhealláin*, Ó Donnchadha (1931: 40).

[25] 'Colonel Henry O'Neill's relation of transactions of General Owen [O']Neill and his party', Gilbert (1879–80, 3/2: 205).

[26] *Aphorismical discovery of treasonable faction*, Gilbert (1879–80, 1/1: 116).

[27] *Cín lae Uí Mhealláin*, Ó Donnchadha (1931: 42), 'Maghnas Ua Domhnaill, son of Niall Garbh and ... were killed'.

[28] *Commentarius Rinuccinianus*, Kavanagh (1932–49, 2: 243), 'Of the Catholics, the Nuncio records only 70 killed and 100 wounded, [none of note] except Maghnas Ó Domhnaill'.

Aodh Buidhe son of Toirdhealbhach

The next Ó Domhnaill leader to emerge in sources outside of the poetry is Toirdhealbhach's son, Aodh Buidhe. It is likely that the regiment of which he became colonel was the same as the one which Maghnas had commanded, but it is also possible that more than one Ó Domhnaill regiment existed or that some Ó Domhnaill contingents fought in other regiments.

Aodh Buidhe is twice named as an insubordinate officer in Eóghan Ruadh's Ulster army. The first time is during the short-lived Kilbeggan mutiny in 1647:

> the supreme council ... prevailed at last with O Neill to alter his former resolutions, and march back to Killbeggan, much against his own and his officers inclinations, some whereof mutynied in four or five days after, and kept their cabal meetings within Killbegan church. The chiefe ringleaders colonel Alexander M'Donnell, Rory Maguire, Hugh Boy O Donnell, with most of the whole army of foot, except ...[29]

The second is the next year, when he and many of his fellow officers deserted Eóghan Ruadh and joined the Royalist faction, under the Lord Lieutenant, Ormond:

> Ormond, Inchiquin, and the supreme council, having agreed about the latter end of spring, Sir Phelim O Neill, lord Iveagh, ... Hugh Boy O Donnell, ... and such other officers as were possessed of their estates in 1641, deserted O Neill, and joined Ormond, Inchiquin, and the supreme council, except ...[30]

He brought 1,200 soldiers with him. As the Confederate Commissioners wrote to Ormond in February 1649:

> Collonell Hugh Boy O Donell, in pursueance of a capitulacion made with him ..., hath ... brought into this Countie twealfe hundred foote from Owen ONeill.[31]

The commissioners intended that six hundred of these were to be billeted on the populace and the remainder disbanded, but it is unclear if any were demobilised.

---

[29] 'Colonel Henry O'Neill's relation', Gilbert (1879–80, 3/2: 206).
[30] 'Colonel Henry O'Neill's relation', Gilbert (1879–80, 3/2: 207–208).
[31] Confederate Commissioners to Ormond, 3 February 1649, Gilbert (1879–80, 1/2: 767).

Aodh Buidhe's relationship with his new masters seems to have been an uneasy one. For instance, Ormond instructs him on 30 August 1649 to 'delay your obedience to our orders noe longer' and not 'to expect to be your own paymaster'.[32] The day before, the gentry of King's Co. had written to Ormond reminding him of payments they had been required to make to:

> Colonel my Lord Digby's regiment of horse, Colonel Hugh Boy O'Donnell and the Lord of Iveagh's regiment of foot and others designed by your Excellency, a far greater sum than is due or payable by this county for many weeks to come[33]

Somhairle Mac an Bhaird's elegy on Aodh Buidhe, *Neart gach tíre ar Thír Chonaill*,[34] does not give much detail on its subject's military career, other than to say that he fought in every corner of Ireland (quatrains 19–23). However, it does give the year of his death as 1649 (quatrain 69) and it tells us that he died in Wexford:

> Tuitis le Gallaibh ghuirt Néill
> i Loch Garman – gníomh aigmhéil! –
> sé fa úr ann ní[or] saoileadh;
> Dún na nGall dá ghnáthchaoineadh.

> He fell at the hands of the foreigners of Niall's field in Wexford – a harsh deed!; it was not imagined that he would be buried there; Donegal is constantly lamenting him. (q. 55)

There can be little doubt that he died when Cromwell stormed Wexford in October 1649. A contemporary account by a British officer states that Ormond had recently sent Aodh Buidhe and others to hold the town:

> Now we will return to Drogheda, into which Crumwell placed a Garrison, and then marched as we said before, to Wexford, wherein was commanded by the Lord Lieutenant, about a fortnight before, the Lord Iveagh's Regiment of Foot, and Collonel Hugh Boy MacTerlagh MacCavra O'Donnell's Regiment, both consisting of about One thousand of Ulster men, together with about One hundred Horse, under whose command I had no Account of;[35]

---

[32] Ormond to Colonel Hugh Boy O'Donell, 30 August 1649, Gilbert (1879–80, 2/2, 452–453).

[33] Petition of the gentry of King's Co. to Ormond, 29 August 1649, Falkiner (1902: 131–132).

[34] Mac Cárthaigh (1999).

[35] *The history of the warr*, Hogan (1873: 90–91).

Here is what his elegist says about the circumstances of his death:

> Bíodh go dtarla an tan-sa i mbroid,
> locthar leis bheith 'na bhrághaid
> 'gun ealbha aing[h]idhe a-mháin
> d'ainmhire meanma an mhacáimh.

> Although at this stage he happened to be in captivity, he rejected being held prisoner by the wicked flock alone [and by no more worthy adversary]; such was the youth's impetuousness of spirit. (q. 53)

This might mean that he was killed while escaping or, with a tweaking of the translation (from 'in captivity' to 'trapped'), it might just mean that he refused to surrender. Either would fit with the next part of the British officer's account:

> where as soon as Crumwell came, he sent them a Trumpet to offer Conditions, which was denied with great Resolution. On which he fell to his Batteries, and made great Breaches in two several places in the Wall, and then assaulted and [was] beaten off, and assaulted again with courage and fury, and entered the Town; where again the fight was renewed, and continued till those within were hacked down, and some of them, endeavouring to escape, were lost without mercy.[36]

An Calbhach Ruadh and Seaán

Whether or not Aodh Buidhe had had sole command over a single unified Ó Domhnaill regiment, some of the family's forces certainly survived after the Wexford defeat. Aodh Buidhe's father, Toirdhealbhach, presumably leader of his branch of the dynasty, fought on. (More of him below.) So too did at least two representatives of the branch from which Maghnas (son of Niall Garbh son of Conn) had come – An Calbhach Ruadh (son of Maghnas son of Conn Óg son of Conn) and Seaán (son of Aodh Buidhe son of Conn).

'Calvagh ODonell' and 'Iohn ODonell' were among the leaders in the newly reunited Ulster army who endorsed 'The declaracion of the nobility, gentry, and comaunders of his Majesty's forces of the province of Ulster' in May 1650,[37] just weeks before the destruction of that army at Scarriffhollis.

---

[36] *The history of the warr*, Hogan (1873: 91).
[37] Gilbert (1879–80, 2/2: 418–20).

Very little other information about An Calbhach during the war years is to be found. He is given the title 'Colonel' by his contemporary, the genealogist An Dubháltach Mac Fhir Bhisigh,[38] but none of the nine poems composed in his praise give concrete details of his military career.[39] However, some at least indicate that he was a soldier, as in these lines from *Treóin an cheannais clann Dálaigh* by Gofraidh Óg Mac an Bhaird:

> Dearna c[h]orcra ó chaitheamh sleagh,
> bráighe d[h]onn ó dhath máilleadh,
> méin rathmhur c[h]ródha chaithmheach
> ónna at[h]lamh ionnsuightheach.

> [He has] a crimson palm from casting spears, a rust-coloured neck from the colour of [chain-mail] links, [and] a successful, brave, generous, gentle, quick, warlike disposition.[40]

Seaán is depicted as an upholder of the faith and addressed as *airgtheoir na n-ainchreidmheach* (line 40b, 'destroyer of the unbelievers') in an anonymous and undated poem to him, *Cóir súil le seasamh Gaoidheal*.[41] He is also likened in an apologue to the man who threw the first spear in the civil war between Caesar and Pompey.[42] All of this would fit well with the split in the Confederation in 1646 between the papal nuncio Rinuccini (backed by the Ulster army) and the supporters of the First Ormond Peace, or indeed with the conflict between the nuncio (again with Eóghan Ruadh's support) and the Supreme Council in 1648.

In *Do dúisgeadh gaisgeadh Gaoidheal*,[43] Gofraidh Óg Mac an Bhaird credits Seaán with bringing the war to Dublin, and I think this most likely to be a reference to the abortive advance against the city later in 1646, after the split. However, it might also refer to the 1649 attack on Dublin under Ormond's command, in which there was at least some Ó Domhnaill involvement:[44]

---

[38] Ó Muraíle (2003, 1: §154.4).

[39] For a list of the nine poems, see Walsh (1948–57, 2: 149–155); see also Mac Cárthaigh (2015: 59).

[40] Mac Cárthaigh (forthcoming: q. 15).

[41] McManus and Ó Raghallaigh (2010: poem 110).

[42] For a full edition and translation of the apologue, see Ó Háinle (2015: 103–115).

[43] Mac Cárthaigh (2016).

[44] Toirdhealbhach Ruadh son of Maghnas Óg son of Aodh Dubh died on that occasion (see below).

> As é tug teannál teintigh
> ó chuan Doire daingeintigh –
> sgél bhus fiach go bráth ar bail –
> go hÁth Cliath agá cabhair.

> It is he who brought flaming battle from the harbour of firm and
> solid Derry to Dublin in a bid to help her – something that, for
> success (?), will be a debt forever. (q. 23)

Seaán was one of a 1648 list of Ulster leaders seen by the Royalist
Ormond faction as potential defectors from Eóghan Ruadh's
Ulster army:

> Jhon Mac Hue Boy ODonell, Torlach ODonell, Mulmory Mac
> Swine and Ereuon Mac Swine may haue or be put in a way to gett
> and inioy, like Knights and skuires, esstats in the county of
> Donegale.[45]

Unless 'Torloch' had parted ways with his son, Aodh Buidhe, this
might predate the latter's defection, discussed above.

Gofraidh Óg's elegy on Seaán, *Do toirneadh ceannas
chlann gCuinn*,[46] says that he fought throughout Ireland in the
course of the war:

> Minic do-rad ruathar niadh
> timcheall Éireann 's gach éinrian;
> dob f[h]iú a bháidh le cloinn cCobhthaigh
> ag roinn áig[h] ar allmhurchaibh.

> Often did he make a martial foray around Ireland in every
> direction; great was his love for Cobhthach's family as he dealt
> out battle to foreigners. (q. 54)

The manner of his death is left open to interpretation:

> Ní[o]r s[h]aoil misi, 's ní mé a-mháin,
> go b[h]fuigheadh caomhfhlaith Chruacháin
> bás acht d'airmreannaibh fhian [n]Gall
> fa bhailbheanguibh fhiadh n-eachtran[n].

> I—and I am not the only one—did not think that Cruachán's
> handsome lord would meet his death in any other way than by the
> spearpoints of bands of foreigners, [fighting] over the calm
> territories of foreigners' lands. (q. 52)

---

[45] Gilbert (1879–80, 1/2: 759).
[46] Mac Cárthaigh (2019).

His death seems to be dated to 1655 but, due to a textual difficulty, this is also uncertain:[47]

> Sé chéd déag bliad[h]ain b[h]uan
> cúig is caoga le comhluadh
> ó theacht d'oighir Dé 'nar ndál
> go a oidhidh, [is] sé ar Seaán.

> Sixteen hundred lasting years (?), adding another fifty five, from the coming of God's heir to us until our Seaán's death. (q. 57)

Toirdhealbhach son of Cathbharr

Toirdhealbhach, first encountered above in 1641, in the very early days of the war, lived until at least 1655. We know this from a poem to him by Cú Choigcríche Ó Cléirigh, *Mo mhallacht ort, a shaoghail*,[48] when the poet praises him for the protection he gave his followers during fourteen years of wartime:

> Do chosain tú íad amhlaidh
> re ré an chogaidh chatharmaigh –
> ceithre bliadhna doirbhe dég
> nar léigis faill 'na ccoimhéd.

> You protected them like that throughout the battle-weaponed war – fourteen trying years during which you never failed to watch over them. (q. 29)

The poet also refers to Toirdhealbhach's surrender at the end of the war:

> Rugais leat fós iar gach seal
> iad uile ag dol fa dhligheadh,
> gor sgaoilsead siar agus soir
> ag port Éirne fad lámhaibh.

> Also, after everything, you brought them all with you when submitting, until they scattered west and east at Erne port under your care. (q. 32)

In the Westminster parliament's 'Act for the Setling of Ireland' (August 1652), 'Tirlogh mac Caffry O Donnel' is among those declared to 'be excepted from pardon for Life and Estate'.[49] We

---

[47] This is because the first line in the quatrain is one syllable short.
[48] Mac Cárthaigh (2013).
[49] Firth and Rait (1911: 599–600).

know that his small estate on the Fanad peninsula in Co. Donegal was confiscated,[50] but was his life spared?

It would seem that he was in prison when *Mo mhallacht ort, a shaoghail* was composed. It is true that the following quatrain could be interpreted as referring to past, rather than current, incarceration:

> Crádh liom do g[h]eimhliughadh daor
> 's gan tadhall duit ar mhíothaom
> acht fíorfhuath, mur tá re treall,
> eachtrann ar uaislibh Éireann.

> A torment to me your being basely chained although the only crime you are familiar with is the bitter hatred harboured of late by foreigners for the nobles of Ireland. (q. 14)

However, another quatrain seems definitely to place him in prison at the time of composition:

> Tabhair foigheidin id bhroid;
> gabh comhairle ó gach caroid;
> dá bhfuilnge martra gan choir,
> buaine dhuit beatha shuthoin.

> Have patience in your captivity; accept advice from every friend; if, free of sin, you suffer martyrdom, eternal life will be all the more lasting for you. (q. 17)

Toirdhealbhach must still have been alive after the Cromwellian period if it is true that a son of his, who brought the Cathach to the Continent, 'died without issue, in his 70th year, at Saint-Germain-en-Laye in 1735'.[51]

Other O'Donnells active in the war

A brother of Toirdhealbhach's, Neachtain, was injured at the battle of Glenmaquin in June 1642:

> Some time in this interval Sir Phelim was routed at Glanmaquin, (on a winter frosty morning) in the county of Donegall, where Alexander M'Colle, his brother Engus, and Nectan O Donnell, Fitz Cathbarr, Fitz Hugh Oge, Fitz Hugh Duff were wounded, Sir Phelim and Alexander M'Colle being ill provided for any action.[52]

---

[50] Simington (1937: 130).
[51] Gilbert (1874: 585).
[52] 'Colonel Henry O'Neill's relation', Gilbert (1879–80, 3/2: 197).

A first cousin of theirs, Toirdhealbhach Ruadh, also fought in the war. This was *Toirdealbach Ruadh mac Maghnuis Óig m. Aodha m. Aodha Duib I Dhomhnaill*.[53] He is named in the 1641 depositions, for instance as 'Tirloghe Roe o donnell (a Captain and great Rebell of Gorttenottera gent'.[54] After the war, 160 acres at 'Gortnottragh' which had belonged to 'Torlagh Ro Mc Manus og O Donell Irish Papist' were confiscated.[55] Following the Restoration, a petition by his son, 'Manus O'Donnell', for the return of that land includes the information that 'His father was killed captain under the Duke of Ormond at Dublin defeat',[56] presumably referring to the 'Battle of Rathmines' in 1649.

It is possible that 'Captaine Manus Mac Egnahan ô Donnell', who is reported to be fighting in Sligo alongside other 'Ulster Rogues' in October 1642,[57] was another first cousin, as Toirdhealbhach's father had a brother named Éigneachán.[58]

Doimnic Ó Domhnaill, brother of Seaán, son of Aodh Buidhe son of Conn, may also have been active in the war. In the poem *Gabhla Fódla fuil Chonaill*,[59] Gofraidh Óg Mac an Bhaird certainly depicts him as a man with military experience:

> Do féchadh a lámh leabhar
> a ttreasuibh gan tuirsioghadh,
> comhghlac do chinn ar gac[h] coir
> tar Chormac le linn Lughaidh.

> His graceful hand has been tested without weakening in battles, a hand that has overcome every crime, surpassing Cormac in Lughaidh's time. (q. 52)

---

53 Ó Muraíle (2003, 1: §154.6).
54 Clarke *et al.* (2014: 242).
55 Simington (1937: 134).
56 Mahaffy (1905: 124).
57 Anon. (1643a: 38).
58 Walsh (1948–57, 2: 196).
59 Mac Cárthaigh (2020).

REFERENCES

Anon., 1643a: *Another extract of more letters sent out of Ireland, informing the condition of the kingdome as it now stands* (London).
—, 1643b: *Speciall good news from Ireland, being a true relation of a late and great victory obtained against the rebels in the north of Ireland: by that pious, prudent, and couragious commander, Sir Will: Stewart, Col.* (London).
—, 1645: *The information of Sir Frederick Hammilton, Knight, and Colonell, given to the Committee of Both Kingdoms, concerning Sir William Cole, Knight, and Colonell; with the scandalous answer of the said Sir William Cole, Knight; together with ...* (London).
Breatnach, Pádraig A., 1994–95: 'The Second Earl of Tyrconnell, †1642', *Éigse* 28, 169–171.
Casway, Jerrold, 1987: 'Mary Stuart O'Donnell', *Donegal annual* 39, 28–38.
Clarke, Aidan, *et al.*, 2014: *1641 depositions, 3, Antrim, Derry, Donegal, Down and Tyrone* (Dublin).
Dillon, Charles, 1995–96: 'Cín lae Uí Mhealláin: Friar O Mellan journal', *Dúiche Néill* 10, 130–207.
Falkiner, Caesar Litton, 1902: *Calendar of the manuscripts of the Marquess of Ormonde, K.P., preserved at Kilkenny Castle*, vol. 1 (London).
Fane, William Dashwood, 1888: *The manuscripts of the Earl Cowper, K.G. preserved at Melbourne Hall, Derbyshire*, vol. 2 (London).
Firth, C.H., and Rait, R.S., 1911: *Acts and ordinances of the interregnum, 1642–1660*, vol. 2, *Acts and ordinances from 9th February, 1649, to 16th March, 1660* (London).
Gilbert, John T., 1874: 'The psalter styled Cathach ascribed to Saint Columba. Sir Richard O'Donnell, Bart., Newport, Co. Mayo, Ireland', *Appendix to the 4th report of the Historical Manuscripts Commission* (London), 584–588.
—, 1879–80: *A contemporary history of affairs in Ireland from 1641 to 1652*, 3 vols (Dublin).
Hogan, Edmund, 1873: *The history of the warr of Ireland from 1641 to 1653. By a British officer, of the regiment of Sir John Clottworthy* (Dublin).
Jennings, Brendan, 1941: 'The career of Hugh, son of Rory O Donnell Earl of Tirconnel, in the Low Countries, 1607–1642', *Studies* 30, 219–234.

Kavanagh, Stanislaus, 1932–49: *Commentarius Rinuccinianus*, 6 vols (Dublin).

Mac Cárthaigh, Eoin, 1999: 'Marbhna ar Aodh Buidhe Ó Domhnaill (†1649)', *Ériu* 50, 41–78.

—, 2002: '*Dia libh, a uaisle Éireann* (1641)', *Ériu* 52, 89–121.

—, 2012: 'Tinn liom do mhaoith, a Mháire', in Eoin Mac Cárthaigh and Jürgen Uhlich (eds), *Féilscríbhinn do Chathal Ó Háinle* (Indreabhán), 159–186.

—, 2013: '*Mo mhallacht ort, a shaoghail* (*c.* 1655): dán is a sheachadadh', *Ériu* 63, 41–77.

—, 2015: 'Gofraidh Óg Mac an Bhaird cecinit: 1. *Deireadh flaithis ag féin Gall*', *Ériu* 65, 57–86.

—, 2016: 'Gofraidh Óg Mac an Bhaird cecinit: 2. *Do dúisgeadh gaisgeadh Gaoidheal*', *Ériu* 66, 77–109.

—, 2017: 'Gofraidh Óg Mac an Bhaird cecinit: 3. *As truagh cor chríche Banbha*', *Ériu* 67, 99–139.

—, 2019: 'Gofraidh Óg Mac an Bhaird cecinit: 4. *Do toirneadh ceannas chlann gCuinn*', *Ériu* 69, 81–125.

—, 2020: 'Gofraidh Óg Mac an Bhaird cecinit: 5. *Gabhla Fódla fuil Chonaill*', *Ériu* 70, 119–170.

—, forthcoming: 'Gofraidh Óg Mac an Bhaird cecinit: 7. *Treóin an cheannais clann Dálaigh*'.

McManus, Damian and Ó Raghallaigh, Eoghan, 2010: *A bardic miscellany: Five hundred bardic poems from manuscripts in Irish and British libraries* (Dublin).

Mahaffy, Robert Pentland, 1900: *Calendar of the state papers relating to Ireland, of the reign of Charles I: 1625–1632* (London).

—, 1901: *Calendar of the state papers relating to Ireland, of the reign of Charles I: 1633–1647* (London).

—, 1905: *Calendar of the state papers relating to Ireland preserved in the Public Record Office: 1660–1662* (London).

Ó Donnchadha, Tadhg, 1931: 'Cín lae Ó Mealláin', *Analecta Hibernica* 3, 1–61.

O Donovan, John, 1856: *Annála Ríoghachta Éireann: Annals of the Kingdom of Ireland by the Four Masters*, 7 vols (Dublin).

Ó Háinle, Cathal, 2015: 'Three apologues and *In Cath Catharda*', *Ériu* 65, 87–126.

Ó Muraíle, Nollaig, 2003: *Leabhar Mór na nGenealach: the Great Book of Irish Genealogies compiled (1645–66) by Dubhaltach Mac Fhirbhisigh*, 5 vols (Dublin).

Russell, Charles W. and Prendergast, John P., 1880: *Calendar of the state papers relating to Ireland, of the reign of James I: 1615–1625* (London).

Simington, Robert C., 1937: *The Civil Survey A.D. 1654–1656*, vol. 3, *Counties of Donegal, Londonderry and Tyrone* (Dublin).

Walsh, Paul, 1933: *Gleanings from Irish manuscripts* (2nd edn, Dublin).

—, 1948–57: *Beatha Aodha Ruaidh Uí Dhomhnaill: The Life of Aodh Ruadh Ó Domhnaill*, 2 vols (London & Dublin).